MASTERS OF WORLD PAINTING

Alexei Venetsianov

AURORA ART PUBLISHERS · LENINGRAD

COMPILED AND INTRODUCED BY DMITRY SARABYANOV
TRANSLATED FROM THE RUSSIAN BY CHRISTINA STAROS
DESIGNED BY DMITRY BIURGANOVSKY

© Aurora Art Publishers, Leningrad, 1988
PRINTED AND BOUND IN THE USSR

$$\text{B } \frac{4903020000\text{-}673}{023(01)\text{-}88}\text{без объявления}$$

ISBN 5-7300-0154-1

In the history of Russian art there have been artists whose names, once disregarded or forgotten, have gradually acquired significance, finally gaining recognition. This is exactly what befell Alexei Venetsianov. His artistic fate, the fate of an unassuming and quiet person who, though troubled by his non-recognition never sought glory, is an illustration of slow continuous advancement, permanency and devotion to the habitual.

During his lifetime the artist was assigned a rather unostentatious place by art critics of the period. The title "Father of Russian genre painting" in those days was not very prestigious. Some time later, after the artist's death, he was denied even that, which is evident from the restrained appraisal of Venetsianov's endeavours given by Vladimir Stasov, the leading critic of the second half of the nineteenth century. It was only at the turn of the century, when the members of the World of Art group and first and foremost Alexander Benois "rediscovered" Venetsianov, that the artist's slow but steady ascension to the summit of glory began.

In the introduction to the catalogue of the 1976 Paris exhibition of Russian Painting of the Epoch of Romanticism, the French art historian Michel Laclotte, when speaking about the picture *Harvesting: Summer*, compared Venetsianov with Pietro della Francesco and the Le Nain brothers.[1] Such a comparison would sound immodest if it were made by a fellow countryman, but in this case it attested to the astonishment of an expert on European painting who awoke to one of the wonders of Russian art.

This amazement is akin to that experienced by Western art historians a few decades ago when they discovered the brilliance of old Russian icon painting, particularly the works of Andrei Rublev.

A whole epoch lies between the discovery of Benois and that of Laclotte, during which Venetsianov's artistic heritage was being evaluated by art critics.[2] But apparently a good many years more will have to go by before Venetsianov takes his proper place in the history of world painting.

It was not accidental that Rublev's name was referred to in context with Venetsianov's. Far from comparing these two masters, I feel, nevertheless, that they both turned out to be exponents of the national qualities in Russian art and both conveyed certain permanent features inherent in Russian outlook and insight, in the Russian concept of the world and experience of living in it. Beyond doubt, we will not find in Venetsianov's works all the formulas of the national artistic spirit, but there are quite a number of them. His work does not contain all the principles of artistic evolution, but several of them, the most important ones for ascertaining general national developmental trends.

At the same time, not all the traditions consolidated in Venetsianov's works have retained at further stages of the development of Russian art. The ones that were in fact actualized, consciously or subconsciously, in the works of Russian artists of the second half of the nineteenth and twentieth centuries seem to be extremely significant for the national artistic self-consciousness.

Along with many other Russian artists, Venetsianov was "awaiting his hour". It was as if he had been born before his time and came into his own only at the mature age of forty. During the years of "waiting" the artist experienced a passion for romantic portraiture and showed a great interest in caricature, which, as some art critics presume, determined his future, as it was in caricature that he first encountered reality. Venetsianov also tried his hand at historical painting, untypical of his endowment. But everywhere he was out of his element: romantic exaltation was foreign to his temperament; caricature held him away from the poetic contemplation so characteristic of the artist's perception of life; the historical genre, though attracting the artist from time to time, also remained alien to him. He was born for genre painting, and the latter was biding its time. But it simply could not establish itself in patriarchal eighteenth-century Russia: the country had not matured enough in those days to be able to glance at the world around without preconception, to perceive the meaning of the most commonplace.

It was only in the 1820s when the sufferings of the Patriotic War of 1812 had been left behind and the pathos of the victory over Napoleon's army had been waning that Russian artists turned for subjects to everyday life.

This belated budding determined peculiarities of genre painting. Having emerged after other artistic branches, it absorbed some of their characteristic features in the process of its establishment: it retained the elements of portrait, landscape and still-life paintings which were fused in Venetsianov's and later in his students' genre pieces.

The state of suspense experienced by Venetsianov (and genre painting as a whole) was highly characteristic of nineteenth-century Russian artists. As no other national art school, the Russian school was bound by the "law of generations" that allotted to each and every phenomenon a definite period of time in history and resolutely terminated it when the necessity for it wore off. This rule sprang from the synthetic character of Russian culture that did not tolerate the isolated existence of painting and literature from each other, from real life, from the spiritual consciousness of the nation. A community of various spiritual activities united around life's principle endeavours persisted in Russia to

Portrait of a Young Man in Spanish Costume. 1804
Pastel on paper. 55×47 cm
The Russian Museum, Leningrad

a greater degree than in other countries. This spiritual oneness begot Rublev's icons after the Kulikovo Battle [3], the genius of Pushkin at the time of Russia's cultural self-determination, Dostoyevsky's tragedy at the time of her spiritual confusion. Venetsianov's name would perhaps be inappropriate in this list of the most eminent. But his revelation of the simple world was also predetermined by the same will of the all-embracing spiritual existence.

The moment of the formation and initial development of Russian genre painting coincided with the time of the European artistic style which, having originated in Germany, was given the name *biedermeier* (nowadays termed Early Realism in West-European art literature) and spread mainly throughout Northern Europe and to some extent in France and England. But the Russian *biedermeier* represented by Tropinin, Venetsianov and his numerous followers did not find clear expression. In Russia it did not exist independently but attached itself to the contemporary trends, Classicism and Romanticism. Here Venetsianov again found himself in a situation so typical of Russia. Owing to the unevenness of its development, to the leaps and halts that it made, Russian culture was frequently compelled to combine the past and the future. Rublev and Dionysius, restrained by medieval artistic mentality, in a way anticipated the Renaissance; likewise, Russian Baroque in eighteenth-century architecture merged into Rococo. Venetsianov's works reflected the intricate interlacing of Classicism, Romanticism and Early Realism on Russian soil and laid down the basic line of development of genre painting. As it often occurred in the history of nineteenth-century art, Venetsianov seemed to have taken advantage of the non-antagonistic co-existence of different trends: he conjoined Classicist concept of the world's equilibrium with an ingenuous poetic comprehension of real life's beauty.

Venetsianov's personal nature proved to be in full harmony with the general course of artistic evolution. With all his heart he plunged into the everyday life of his rural community; he was almost engulfed by this provincial daily life, but the deeper the artist rooted himself in it, the more resolutely did he strive to preserve the lucidity of his vision, the ability to discern in a commonplace event the deeper meaning: the continuous round of life, the indissoluble unity of man and nature. In this way the Classical component of Venetsianov's genre painting fused with the artist's mode of life and his daily inclinations.

Above we have already noted the composite character of Venetsianov's art, meaning the blending of elements of different trends in genre painting. This fusing, displayed in various forms, along with the synthesis of different stylistic veins, indicates the syncretism so characteristic of many stages of the development of Russian culture. The most stable in this syncretic unity were the traditional national ties that developed independently of the artist's will, at times linking the distant past with the present and making their way through various trends and veins depending exclusively on their own force.

Since the time of Russian icon painting a case of such profound contemplative poetic perception of life had been unknown to art. It was by this contemplation that harmony in the artistic image was achieved. Not by improving the reality as the artists of Classicism used to do, nor by difficult solution of conflict, which was characteristic of Alexander Ivanov, nor by catharsis in the dénouement of tragedy, as was often done by the Romantics, but by direct contemplation of verity and beauty.

Daily occurrences assume somewhat idealized features in Venetsianov's conception; they are arranged in certain thematic groups. Among these the artist fixes his attention on the most important thing, from his point of view — on nature in its primary aspect: on sky and earth, on mother and child, incarnating in their union the idea of continuation of life, and, lastly, on the human abode. In the artist's contemplation, the world is seen as a diminutive model of the universe, and man becomes an exponent of mankind as a whole.

All the peculiarities of Venetsianov's art are rooted in this stand of his. The chosen themes and motifs, the characters, their conduct and movement, the composition, the treatment of light and colour — all rest on it. This dependence is sustained by Venetsianov's relative freedom of action. Naturally, the artist was not completely free as he was committed to the process of natural development of Russian painting, but as an innovator, as the actual proponent of a new stage in Russian painting he possessed considerable freedom of choice.

Venetsianov selected his themes and motifs out of what life granted him. In the process of work he recreated them, by staging the scene, when possible, and placing the characters in appropriate places. In the painting *Threshing Floor*, Venetsianov's first programmatic work, the performance of the actor-models is especially noticeable. This was just the way professors in Academy studios arranged in front of their students the models in appropriate attitudes and attires, who posed as Biblical characters or heroes from Russian history. Later the models' acting becomes better concealed from the viewer not because of more skilful acting, but because the artist had achieved a more natural interpretation of the scene. Venetsianov's models impersonated themselves[4] and this explains the organic integrity reached by the artist in his peasant paintings.

Venetsianov's canvases show the most natural activities. His characters work and rest, mothers nurse their sucklings, children play; that is, they expose their nature in a most ingenuous way. These simple actions do not allow the possibility of a conflict. They exist out of time, they do not suggest any development. But sometimes Venetsianov seemingly gives a hint of the possibility of their development in time. In the painting *Harvesting: Summer*, two children are standing near a mother breastfeeding her baby. Quite possibly they had brought the infant and are now waiting to carry it away. But Venetsianov could have done without this justification of the main motif. He is not interested in the action itself, but in something already developed and accomplished, something having a complete integral embodiment. It seems as if the artist thinks in fixed and invariable formulas.

In the painting *In the Field: Spring*, the woman leading the horse by the bridle lightly treads barefoot on the ploughed ground. Just for a moment she has turned her head to glance at her child sitting at the edge of the field nearby. This does not destroy the persistent motif characteristic of Venetsianov's work. Mainly thanks to the efforts of Venetsianov and his students, a number of such formula-motifs were devised in the 1820s—1840s: a peasant woman with a sickle, yoke, scythe or rake, a peasant putting on bast shoes, an adolescent with an axe, a woman with a child in her arms, a small child with a cat, a boy fishing, a carpenter planing a board.

This approach to subject or motif is well-known. In Dutch and Flemish eighteenth-century genre painting we also find subjects of semblance: Dutch courtyards, scenes showing card playing or scuffles in a tavern, playing music or a doctor's visit. But while in Dutch and Flemish paintings all these subject patterns were mainly taken from mythological and allegorical sources and tended to diversification within each pattern, in

Portrait of Vera Putiatina. Second half of the 1810s
Oil on panel. 30×23.5 cm
The Tretyakov Gallery, Moscow

the works of Venetsianov and his students they, by contrast, were seemingly concentrated on their own essence. Equally precise were the gestures of Venetsianov's personages. They are quite demonstrative and explicit. The artist attached great importance to the poses of the figures and the turns of the heads. This plastic motif is manifested in Venetsianov's paintings more than in any other nineteenth-century master's works, maybe with the exception of Alexander Ivanov.

The hand movements of Venetsianov's characters are nearly always functional. In his paintings hands hold a bridle, carry an earthenware pot, grasp a sickle or an axe, hold out a hunk of bread or show mushrooms that have been picked. Even in his *Sleeping Shepherd Boy*, where the plot does not require any hand movement, the artist turned the left palm of the boy in an inquiring gesture. Only in his first composition on a peasant theme (*Peeling Beets*) the artist does not seem to know what to do with the hands and placed them too close to each other in an awkward disharmony on a small part of the pictorial surface. Venetsianov's contemplative poesy does not stand any bustle and endures it even less when the plot unfolds gradually.

The peculiarity of Venetsianov's creative method lies in the fact that he never ranked a life drawing

Reaper. Not later than 1826
Oil on canvas. 30×24 cm
The Russian Museum, Leningrad

with a completed picture. It is suffice to compare his mature genre canvases of the 1820s with sketches from life of the same period or with variants of the composition *Life-drawing Class at the Academy of Arts* to become convinced of the great difference between them. In his drawings the artist freely captures everyday scenes, catching people in random poses, and that is why they lack genuine Venetsianov-like traits. If you lay them next to the drawings of his contemporary artists, the comparison will prove to be unfavourable, and they will fade without revealing their flavour.

Although he declared the principle of painting *à la nature* and seemingly had taken François Marius Granet's *Interior of the Choir of the Capuchin Church in Piazza Barberini in Rome* as an example, Venetsianov actually interpreted the principle of naturalness in his own way and digressed from the naturalistic manner of the French master. Whereas Granet's picture is dominated by the space leading the viewer to the heart of the interior, and the figures are subordinate to this spatial movement and do not comprise the centre of the composition, Venetsianov's composition is fashioned by figures, around which the space is arranged, or, in any case, a certain equilibrium is reached between the space, on the one hand, and the figures or objects, on the other. Only in Venetsianov's first "post-Granet" experiment — the painting *Threshing Floor* — is this balance slightly upset in favour of the space.

At times in Venetsianov's more mature works we can find wide spatial expansion. The painting *Harvesting: Summer* is composed so that special perspective lines — the shadow of the shed and the jutting of the unreaped rye — direct the viewer's eye into the depth of the picture. But then the movement spreads, wending its way not so much to the centre as to the sides. It tends towards the horizontal despite the vertical format of the canvas. The plane of the wooden planking where the peasant woman is sitting is the first to create this impression. Then the lines parallel to the plane seem to flow in waves, now thickening, now thinning and finally reach the horizon. The space is seemingly objectified, the horizontal becomes perceptible: and this is not merely a motif characteristic of Russian flat-country landscape, but a formula peculiar to Russian visual perception.

Here we touch upon an important aspect of Venetsianov's creative work. The artist, who was the first to render on his canvases Russian nature, discovered, probably, its most essential features. In many of his paintings — *In the Field: Spring, Sleeping Shepherd Boy, Peasant Children in the Field, Haymaking* — the artist meticulously elaborates the foreground, painstakingly depicting the ploughed earth, the grasses, stones and leaves. The viewer can almost feel the soil beneath the grassy cover. And then the earth seems to expand to infinity, going beyond the bounds of the pictorial field, unlimited by the coulisses. The earth, its boundlessness is perceived by the artist not as a philosophical category (as with his contemporary Alexander Ivanov) but as a given reality and in addition as the place of man's habitat, the place where he works.

Venetsianov did not paint landscapes as such. He could not conceive of nature apart from man. The images of nature that he created could not be called lyrical. Nature's beauty in his conception is ontological; that is, it does not depend on our perception. It simply exists. It must be discovered and perceived. There is no need to spiritualize it: from the very beginning of its existence every blade of grass, every branch of a tree, every bush has possessed this spirituality. There is no need to compare nature with man's state of mind or to search for an echo of man's mood in nature.

When delineating nature Venetsianov renders its beauty most directly. The artist delights in the summer, the day, the sun, the clear sky with little unpretentious clouds. He is indifferent to sunsets, winds, storms, transitions from one state of weather to another. He prefers the moments when nature is still. Almost all of the artist's pictures are tranquil but sometimes their tranquility is indeed cosmic, as for instance, in the paintings *Sleeping Shepherd Boy* and *Harvesting: Summer*. The beauty of nature is better revealed in stillness: there really must not be anything accidental in it. It should appear to us in its most natural condition. Thus, nature is elucidated in the same way as man, canonically to a certain extent.

Fortune-telling with Cards. 1842
Oil on canvas. 75.5×62 cm
The Russian Museum, Leningrad

Peasant Children in the Field. 1820s
Oil on canvas. 38.5×30 cm
The Russian Museum, Leningrad

Interrelations between man and nature in Venetsianov's works are revealed even in his interiors. In fact, it was with the interiors that Venetsianov started his work — as he himself put it — *à la nature. Threshing Floor, Country-seat Lady's Morning, Country Morning: A Family at Tea* (survives only as a lithograph copy) painted in the early 1820s show the artist's interest in the problem of man and nature and open the prospects for further development of this genre, so popular in the 1820s—1840s. These works were followed by the remarkable interiors of Kapiton Zelentsov, Alexander Alexeyev, Alexei Tyranov, Fiodor Slaviansky, Yevgraf Krendovsky, Grigory Soroka and Fiodor Tolstoi. Venetsianov transformed this genre, having imparted to representation of the interior a totally new meaning in comparison to that which it had had in the art of the eighteenth and early nineteenth centuries. In those days the interior was usually treated as an architectural composition. Palace chambers, broad staircases, picture galleries, huge cathedrals which were always ceremonially arrayed, did not bear the features of an abode. The artists simply did not view them as residential. Venetsianov democratized the genre of the interior and brought it closer to everyday life. However, he did not belittle its significance, as the idea of the family hearth was becoming imbued with elevated meaning.[5]

The Country-seat Lady's Morning most consistently embodies Venetsianov's approach to interior paintings.

The perfect unity of the human, the natural and the material is reached here. Alexander Benois, artist and critic, said the following about this picture: "Venetsianov did cope with the task of communicating in transparent serene tones the difficult effect of a delicate grey light gently flowing through the only window in the back of the room. The skill with which the whole right corner of the room is painted — the wall in the shade, the plaster casts on the tall-boy — is worthy of the most sincere wonderment. And it is executed without any ostentatious tricks. . ."[6]

The perfect rendition of light, the highlights, the reflection in the mirror do not stir up a feeling of unsteadiness, fleetingness, of balancing between the real and the unreal. In Venetsianov's painting all these things belong to the real world, filled with steady and constant beauty. Light is always an integral part of the artist's works, spreading over the rye field in the painting *Summer*, rising to the skies in *Spring*, imbuing each blade of grass with yellowing green in *Sleeping Shepherd Boy*. Already in his early canvases *Threshing Floor* and *Country-seat Lady's Morning*, which still echo Granet's painting, a special role is assigned to the light. But Venetsianov did not want to or was not able to amplify it to a degree that would upset the balance of the world he was creating. Light for him was one of the natural elements. Light does not change the world, but conveys it together with other elements. Light is constant, continuous; in its essence it is the opposite of darkness, which incidentally never occurs in Venetsianov's paintings, while light is always rendered by him as the vivifying source.

It is interesting to compare the view-from-a-window motif in the works of Venetsianov and his followers with that by German Romantic artists.[7] In the picture *Woman by the Window*, painted by Caspar David Friedrich in 1822 — a year before Venetsianov produced his *Country-seat Lady's Morning* — the desire to underline domestic cosiness is not felt; in other words, the German artist is far from the *biedermeier* interpretation of the scene. There are almost no objects in the interior, which has no depth. The window frame, the elongated figure of the woman, the verticals of the sailboat masts are all subordinate to the upward drive to the fascinating sky, to the captivating endless distance. The mystery of this distance, the yearning for boundlessness, the conflict between the finite and the infinite, the insuperability of this conflict are present here.

Venetsianov and his pupils elucidated a similar motif in quite a different way. In their representation the world is uniform. The light pouring through the windows or doors opened into the interior unites man and nature. The walls of the houses present no obstacle. Venetsianov was the first to glance unaffectedly and naively at the natural surrounding through a window or through the open gates of the threshing floor. The bit of scenery visible in those apertures united the interior with the outer world.

Some other peculiarities in devising interior scenes inherent in Russian painting also take shape in Venetsianov's work. His *Threshing Floor* is stretched horizontally from the foreground to the background. In his *Country-seat Lady's Morning* the window on the wall opposite the viewer also enhances the horizontal extension of space. His followers gladly adopted the suite-of-rooms motif for the same purpose. Here once again we encounter the dominance of extension which is manifest in the horizontality of Venetsianov's compositions. It is interesting to note the different interpretation of the chamber motif in German painting: as a rule the rooms present an enclosed space and openings into the landscape or other rooms are not shown.

Today Venetsianov's remarkable role in the history of Russian painting is obvious. The artist opened to art the world of the Russian village, the Russian countryside that had been previously scarcely visible through the veil of artistic conventionality. For many decades Russian painting proceeded along this pathway even though creative methods, attitudes towards the peasantry and the artistic idiom were undergoing changes. Hence, Venetsianov's tradition has survived for a long time in modified form, and it is still alive today.

In analyzing Venetsianov's paintings, I have tried to underline the peculiarities of the national plastic imagery. In this connection there may arise a question: have there been masters in the history of Russian art who expressed the same features, if not so definitely, then at least partially? Russian icon painting in its main aspects gives a positive answer to this question, though I deliberately have not attempted the comparison of those two artistic phenomena. Some points could be found where Venetsianov is in accord with Alexander Ivanov, though the latter did not even recognize genre painting. Both of them, each in his own way, strove to express the essence of being, although one proceeded from everyday life and the other from religion, myth and history. They both explored a direct way from the particular to the general. But that's where the analogies with contemporaries end. Venetsianov's pupils seem to have lost many of their teacher's achievements. Further deviation from his principles is even more evident in later years. In the second half of the nineteenth century only Alexander Morozov, an obscure though attractive artist from the St. Petersburg Artists' Society, and to a lesser degree the Itinerant Vasily Maximov "bear resemblance" to Venetsianov. At the turn of the century memories of Venetsianov were revived in poetic interior scenes by the World of Art artists and the Union of Russian Artists: in peasant paintings by Zinaida Serebriakova and in the works of Kuzma Petrov-Vodkin. The name of Pavel Kuznetsov can also be added to those already mentioned. Most likely, the list of parallels is exhausted here. But there is no doubt that the main features of the national artistic worldview have been communicated in Venetsianov's work.

It is a common thing for a genius to stand alone, because his special creativity is inimitable. The ingenuity of a great national artist can find response beyond the art in which he excelled. Nearly every art historian who has written about Venetsianov, compares the artist with Alexander Pushkin. Indeed, in Pushkin's poem *Eugene Onegin*, Russian seasons of the year, unfolding before us in their traditional forms, bear a resemblance to Venetsianov's representations. The poet recreates nature, the village, the peasants with an exceptional accuracy without sophisticated comparisons and conflicts, by simply giving descriptions of the most natural phenomena of life passed through the "magic crystal" of poetry. Pushkin's unpretentious and artless verses are known to every Russian from childhood, as are Venetsianov's pictures *In the Field: Spring*, and *Harvesting: Summer*. But while in Venetsianov's works the plastic formula of everyday life is expressed only in the poesy of the simple, Pushkin's creative scope is considerably wider.

In comparing Venetsianov with Pushkin, we have exceeded the bounds of painting. And this is not accidental. Venetsianov's work cannot be analyzed only from the point of view of his purely painterly achievements. It is no less important to evaluate the artist from a wider cultural and social standpoint. Venetsianov revealed the human dignity of the common toiler and destroyed the barriers between the estates; he glorified peasant labour and associated his moral ideal with the working man. In his paintings he tackled those vital problems that were agitating Russian society throughout the nineteenth century.

[1] *See*: Michel Laclotte, *La peinture russe à l'époque romantique. Galeries Nationales du Grand Palais*, 1976—1977, p. 8.

[2] An important role in studying Venetsianov's heritage was played by N. Wrangel in the 1910s; by A. Efros and A. Müller in the 1820s—1830s; by T. Alexeyeva, M. Alpatov, N. Kovalenskaya, N. Mashkovtsev, A. Savinov, G. Smirnov, and Z. Fomicheva in subsequent years.

[3] The great battle of Russian regiments with Dmitry Donskoi (of the Don) at their head against Mamai's Mongol-Tartar hordes on September 8, 1380 on the Kulikovo Field. Ended in defeat for the Mongol-Tartars. Prepared the way for the liberation of the Russians and other peoples from the Mongol-Tartar yoke.

[4] Only in his later works, such as *Bacchante* and *Toilet of Diana*, the models play roles foreign to them. In such cases, despite the artist's intentions, the viewer does not see Bacchante or Diana but only the models posing for them.

[5] T. Alexeyeva, "*Venetsianov and the Evolution of Genre Painting*". in: *A History of Russian Art*, vol. 8, book 1, Moscow, 1963, pp. 572—576 (in Russian).

[6] Cited from: E. Logvinskaya, *The Interior in Russian Painting of the First Half of the Nineteenth Century*, Moscow, 1978, p. 42 (in Russian).

[7] In recent decades West-European art criticism touched on this motif repeatedly. For instance, in 1956 an exhibition entitled *View from the Window* was held in Dortmund.

1780	Born February 7 (18 New Style) in Moscow into the family of a second-guild merchant Gavriil Venetsianov. His mother Anna Venetsianova (née Kalashnikova) was also from a merchant-class family.
1790—1800s	After finishing a private boarding school, works as a draughtsman.
1802	Moves to St. Petersburg and works as an assistant land surveyor.
Mid-1800s	Continues to live in St. Petersburg (according to most researchers and biographers). Possibly studies under Vladimir Borovikovsky.
1804	Paints *Portrait of a Young Man in Spanish Costume*.
1807	Enters the service in the office of the Postmaster General.
1808	Begins to put out a *Caricature Magazine* for 1808. His etching *Dignitary* published in the first issue arouses the Emperor's wrath. The magazine is banned by the censor.
1809	Transfers to the Department of State Property. Appointed land surveyor to St. Petersburg province.
1811	Receives the title of Candidate for Academician from the Academy of Arts for his *Self-portrait*. Receives the title of Academician for the *Portrait of Kirill Golovachevsky*.
1812—13	Creates a series of caricatures criticizing Gallomania in Russian Society.
1815	Marries Martha Azaryeva. Buys a small estate in Tver province (now Kalinin region). From this time on to the end of his life, spends summers on his estate and winters in St. Petersburg.
1816	The birth of his daughter Alexandra.
1818	The birth of his daughter Felicia.
1819	Resigning from his formal duties, moves to his estate, where he paints and sets up a school for peasant children.
Late 1810s	Becomes a member of the Society for the Founding of Schools of Reciprocal Training, a legal educational organization of the Decembrists' Union for Prosperity.
1821	Becomes acquainted with François Marius Granet's painting *Interior of the Choir of the Capuchin Church in Piazza Barberini in Rome*. The picture fascinates Venetsianov.
1823	The pastel *Peeling Beets*, completed the previous year, is purchased for the Hermitage. Finishes the *Threshing Floor*. (It was begun, possibly in 1821 after Venetsianov had seen Granet's picture and had been strongly impressed by it.) Completes the painting *Country-seat Lady's Morning*. Supposedly the artist depicted his wife in it.
1824—25	Takes the first pupils, among them Alexei Tyranov and Nikifor Krylov. In twenty years of pedagogical activity, he taught more than seventy pupils, including several serfs. Classes were held both on the artist's estate and in St. Petersburg. Works on his competitive composition for the title of Professor of the Academy of Arts, *Life-drawing Class at the Academy of Arts* (unfinished).
Mid-1820s	Works on his most well-known and significant pictures *Sleeping Shepherd Boy*, *In the Field: Spring*, *Harvesting: Summer*.
1825	Creates his peasant portrait studies *Zakharka*, *Head of an Old Peasant*.
1826	Takes part in the exhibition organized by the Society for the Encouragement of Russian Artists, exhibiting twenty of his paintings and also lithographs from his pictures executed by his pupils.
1827	The Russian Gallery of the Hermitage purchases two of his paintings, including *Sleeping Shepherd Boy*. Participates in the exhibition at the Academy of Arts and receives favourable critical reviews.
1829	Sells part of his estate.
1830	Receives the title of Painter to His Majesty the Emperor. Exhibits at the Academy of Arts. Favourable press reviews. Mortgages the estate.
1831	"Letter to the Editor of the Literary Supplement from Our Well-known Painter A. Venetsianov" is published in the literary supplement to the *Russian Veteran*. A considerable part of the letter is devoted to Franz Krüger's painting *Parade in Berlin*, highly praised by Venetsianov. The artist's wife dies from cholera.

1834	Executes a lithographic portrait of Nikolai Gogol.
Mid-1830s	Writes his theoretical work *Some Notes on Perspective* summing up his experience in creative and pedagogical activities.
1837	Takes part in the first art lottery of the Society for the Encouragement of Russian Artists. The Society buys three of Venetsianov's paintings.
1838	Participates in the second lottery of the Society for the Encouragement of Russian Artists and in the competition at the Academy of Arts for the Anatoly Demidov prize, entering his picture *Peter the Great. The Foundation of St. Petersburg.* Contributes to the emancipation from serfdom of the future eminent Ukrainian writer and artist Taras Shevchenko.
1839	Takes part in the third art lottery of the Society for the Encouragement of Russian Artists and in the benefit lottery for a children's hospital in St. Petersburg. Exhibits at the Academy of Arts. His letter on printing in wax paints, *The Secret of Lipmann's Pictures,* is published in the newspaper *The Northern Bee* (No 276).
Late 1830s—1840s	Writes articles on the system of teaching in drawing classes.
About 1840	Writes his *Autobiographical Note.*
1840—43	Unsuccessfully seeks a professorship at the Academy of Arts or at the Moscow School of Painting and Sculpture.
1840s	Gives lessons to Grigory Soroka, one of his most gifted students, for whose fate the artist displayed deep concern.
1846—47	Receives a commission for painting an iconostasis and the image of St. Macarius for the Church of the Nativity of the Virgin in the Trinity Monastery at Kaliazin. Plans to begin this work.
1847	On December 4 (16) Venetsianov dies. On the way from his estate to Tver, near the village of Poddubye, his horses tore down a steep hill, flinging him out of the cart. Venetsianov died on the spot. Buried in the village of Dubrovskoye, Vyshny Volochok district.

PEELING BEETS. Not later than 1822
Pastel on paper. 58×68 cm
The Russian Museum, Leningrad

THRESHING FLOOR. Between 1821 and 1823
Oil on canvas. 66.5×80.5 cm
The Russian Museum, Leningrad

PEASANT GIRL WITH CORNFLOWERS. 1820s
Oil on canvas. 48.3×37.1 cm
 The Tretyakov Gallery, Moscow

COUNTRY-SEAT LADY'S MORNING. 1823
Oil on panel. 41.5×32.5 cm
The Russian Museum, Leningrad

IN THE FIELD: SPRING. Early 1820s
Oil on canvas. 51.2×65.5 cm
The Tretyakov Gallery, Moscow

HARVESTING: SUMMER. Mid-1820s
Oil on canvas. 60×48.3 cm
The Tretyakov Gallery, Moscow

HEAD OF AN OLD PEASANT. 1825
Oil on canvas. 41×31.5 cm
The Tretyakov Gallery, Moscow

ZAKHARKA. 1825
Oil on cardboard. 39.8×30.7 cm
The Tretyakov Gallery, Moscow

SLEEPING SHEPHERD BOY. Between 1823 and 1826
Oil on panel. 27.5×36.5 cm
The Russian Museum, Leningrad

PORTRAIT OF ALEXANDRA VENETSIANOVA,
THE ARTIST'S DAUGHTER. *Ca.* 1826
Oil on canvas. 41×33 cm
The Tretyakov Gallery, Moscow

REAPERS. Late 1820s
Oil on canvas. 66.7×52 cm
The Russian Museum, Leningrad

PEASANT GIRL WITH A CALF. Late 1820s
Oil on canvas. 65.5×53 cm
The Tretyakov Gallery, Moscow

BATHERS. 1829
Oil on canvas. 52.5×36.5 cm
The Russian Museum, Leningrad

SLEEPING GIRL. 1840s
Oil on canvas. 53.2×68 cm
Art Museum, Gorky